The Paintings of María Izquierdo

The Paintings of María Izquierdo

Blaze Carter

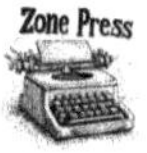
Zone Press

CONTENTS

To Diego Rivera, who recognized a true artist
when he saw one.

María Izquierdo, An Artist of Her Own Making

There are artists whose stories arrive prepackaged: the myth, the suffering, the love affairs that burn fast and blow out even faster, the canvases hauled from obscurity into museum vitrines, the quotes that become slogans on tote bags. And then there are artists like María Izquierdo, who lived her life with such ferocious inwardness that it takes a certain kind of attention—quiet, persistent, almost stubborn—to see her clearly.

You could say she was overshadowed. By Diego, by Frida, by the entire muralist apparatus of the postrevolutionary Mexican state.

But to say she was overshadowed implies she occupied the same stage, and that is only partially true. Izquierdo was both inside and outside, claimed and unclaimed, canon adjacent but unwilling to bend herself into the shape that canon required.

When you look at one of her paintings—say *Sueño y premonición (Dream and Premonition)* from 1947—you don't feel that overwhelming muralist force, the rhetoric turned into plaster. You feel instead an eerie clarity, a woman standing beside her own severed head, a tower in flames. It is the vision of someone who lived with her eyes half turned inward, half toward the desert horizon of her childhood, who refused to be enlisted into the state's idea of Mexican art.

To write about María Izquierdo is, in a way, to write about a kind of refusal.

And yet the story begins not with refusal but with a girl—small, watchful, already half wise—born in 1902 in San Juan de los Lagos, a pilgrimage town in Jalisco where miracles were rumored the way weather is forecast: casually, almost off-hand. Her early life is sometimes described as "provincial," as if this were a limitation.

But the landscape there is not small. The desert skies open like paper torn from both ends. The basilica glitters with a devotional excess that, if you stand too close, overwhelms your sense of proportion. It is not hard to imagine how a child growing up in that town might learn early the relationship between the sacred and the ordinary.

Izquierdo would later say she painted from memories—*real* memories but memories bent into symbols, the way light bends when it meets stained glass.

There are artists whose childhoods you can reconstruct like an archaeological site. Everything is logical, every root visible. María's childhood is harder to chart, partly because she did not speak of it often, and partly because a childhood in rural Mexico at the turn of the century is its own kind of unknowable geography.

Her father died when she was still small. Her mother remarried; her grandfather exerted a strict moral presence. The household was Catholic, disciplined, and—crucially—restless. They moved between Jalisco and Torreón in Coahuila, following work, survival, or perhaps a deeper desire for stability that never quite materialized. The Mexican Revolution, with all its violent promise, curled around the edges of her youth. She was eight when it exploded into full force; she was thirteen when it blew the roof off everyday life entirely.

María did not, as far as anyone knows, paint as a child. She was married off at fourteen—to a military man, a much older one—because that was what was done. This is the part of her biography that is almost always recited quickly, in the hushed tone of inevitability. But imagine fourteen. Imagine the heat of Torreón in summer, the desert wind pushing sand against walls, the sound of boots on a dirt road. Imagine a girl whose entire life had been dictated by others suddenly expected to replicate the rhythms of an adult woman, to produce children, to inhabit a life that seemed to have pre-existed her.

She gave birth to three children by the time she was twenty, and yet this is not the center of her story. It is the preface. A long, slow exhale before the door opens.

In 1923, she did something that even now feels radical: she left.

Not walked away softly. Not drifted apart. She left, with her children, and headed for Mexico City—the capital, the laboratory of modern Mexican identity, the city that promised possibility but rarely delivered it without cost.

This is where María Izquierdo's story finally begins.

In the 1920s, Mexico City was a fever dream. Post-revolutionary nationalism was turning into aesthetic doctrine. The muralists had seized walls the way generals seize territory. Diego Rivera had returned from Europe with enough ambition for five men. José Clemente Orozco burned with fire and skepticism in equal measure. David Alfaro Siqueiros shouted his politics like a sermon.

Into this storm walked María Izquierdo, twenty-one years old, newly separated, carrying three small children and—one imagines—more courage than fear.

No one expected anything from her. She was not connected. She was not trained. She was, perhaps most inconveniently for the gatekeepers, a woman.

And yet, almost immediately, the city cracked open for her.

The first hinge was her enrollment in the Escuela Nacional de Bellas Artes (ENBA), the art academy where, among the men painting the nation's future on scaffolds, she found herself under the instruction of Siqueiros. Siqueiros, for all his flaws—and they were abundant—had a nose for talent. He recognized something in her: a clarity, a directionality that didn't derive from anyone else. He called her the most promising student of her generation.

This should have been the beginning of a straightforward ascent, the kind Rivera enjoyed, the kind Kahlo mythologized. But María was never straightforward.

She lasted only a year at the academy.

There are multiple versions of why. Some say she left because she needed to work. Others say she clashed with the rigid academic hierarchy. Whatever the reason, she walked out the door with the same decisive energy that carried her from her marriage. And, remarkably, she kept painting.

It is here that her work acquires its first recognizable signature: a sense of stillness. While the muralists were painting the revolution in motion—bodies twisting, fists raised, the nation imagined as a muscular collective—Izquierdo painted still lifes, circus performers, devotional altars, women waiting in doorways, and dreams.

She painted the world as if it were holding its breath.

The male critics could not make sense of her. They wanted grand narratives; she gave them quiet symbols. They wanted ideology; she gave them memory. They wanted nationalism; she gave them the personal as political before that phrase was ever coined.

Something in her work unsettled them.

This would become a pattern.

The popular story of Mexican modernism is filled with men and with women who served as their muses, lovers, collaborators, or symbolic foils. But María Izquierdo was nobody's muse. She refused the role.

What she wanted—what she articulated repeatedly in interviews—was simple:
the right of women to create art from their own vision, not from the expectations placed upon them.

In a 1930 interview, she said:

> "It is urgent for us women to break once and for all with the idea that we live only to marry, to have children, and to be servants to men. It is important for women with artistic vocations to dedicate themselves to their work... without fear or prejudice."

This was the kind of statement that made the men around her nervous.

Remember: this was 1930. Kahlo had not yet become the famous *Frida*. The feminist vocabulary we have now did not exist.

But here was María, speaking with the clarity of someone who had already lived through a life she did not choose—and had no intention of repeating that mistake.

At this time she also began a relationship with the painter Rufino Tamayo, who was older, trained in academic techniques, and respected by cultural elites. Their relationship was both personal and artistic; he encouraged her, supported her exhibitions, and helped introduce her to international circles.

But Tamayo was not her Pygmalion. María did not sculpt herself to fit his aesthetic world. If anything, he softened under her influence. Her independence—her refusal to let herself be overshadowed—complicated their partnership, and the relationship eventually dissolved, but the early years provided stability and access.

In 1928, she became the first Mexican woman to have a solo exhibition in the United States. New York critics found her work "emotionally compelling," "pure," "almost religious." The reviews read today like a mixture of admiration and confusion: they could see the power but lacked the cultural vocabulary to place it.

Izquierdo did not help them by providing easy explanations. She spoke of memory, intuition, dreams, altars—words critics could not categorize. They wanted to know what school she belonged to. She insisted she belonged to none.

Independent women make people anxious. Independent women artists make institutions anxious.

And María Izquierdo would soon learn exactly how anxious.

In 1945, the Mexican government commissioned María Izquierdo to paint a large mural at the Palacio del Departamento del Distrito Federal—a historic moment, the *first* time a woman had been granted a major public mural commission.

It should have changed her career.

It should have changed the history of Mexican art.

It should have changed how we talk about women painters in the mid-twentieth century.

Instead, it became a textbook case of institutional sabotage.

Rivera and Siqueiros—her former mentors—objected. Publicly and aggressively. They declared that she lacked the technical skill to complete a large-scale mural. They wrote letters, pulled political strings, and ultimately convinced the government to revoke the commission.

It is difficult to overstate the humiliation of this moment.

She had been chosen.

She had designed the mural.

She had begun the work.

And they took it from her.

It is one thing to face criticism as a painter; it is another to be shut out of the world of monumental public art entirely because the men in charge feared what it would mean to let a woman stand beside them on the wall of history.

Izquierdo responded not with public fury but with a kind of haunted grief. The betrayal left a mark you can see in her later paintings, especially the ones with cut ropes, damaged altars, broken balloons—images of celebration interrupted.

This was, for María, the great wound.

After this scandal, commissions dried up. Exhibitions waned. She kept painting, but with a loneliness that became visible in the work itself.

If you want to understand María Izquierdo, stand in front of "Alegoría del trabajo" (Allegory of Work), or "Niña con bandera", or "Retrato de Belem", or her astonishing series of altars from the early 1940s. In these works, the Mexican home becomes a stage set, the domestic interior burns with the same emotional intensity as the desert. Objects—bridges, horses, papel picado, masks—take on the weight of unsaid things.

Her altar scenes, for example, do not behave like documentary depictions of folk religion. They feel like personal rituals disguised as public ones. The candles flicker with a psychological voltage; the fruits seem to rot just slightly faster than they should. Everything is symbolic but nothing is explained.

Unlike Kahlo, who painted her life as a series of dramatic self-portraits, Izquierdo rarely painted herself directly. She painted instead the world as she felt it: discontinuous, sacred, ominous, beautiful. Her imagination was theatrical in the sense that a stage designer's imagination is theatrical—a world built from memory and metaphor, not autobiography.

The circus paintings—*La Cabalgata, Payasos, Trapecistas*—are perhaps the clearest example. Critics at the time described them as "whimsical," which is a word people often use when they don't understand a woman's complexity.

But these works are not whimsical.

They are devastating. The trapeze artists hang in a space suspended between danger and grace; the clowns wear expressions that hint at exhaustion rather than humor. These are not circus performers; they are metaphors for fragility.

María Izquierdo saw the circus for what it was: a place where bodies perform acts of transcendence under the threat of falling.

So, too, her own life.

In 1948, at the age of forty-six, María suffered a stroke. It partially paralyzed her and limited the movement of her right side.

But she continued to paint, teaching herself to adapt, to work through physical impairment with the same resolve she had used to navigate the art world's gendered limits.

The last years of her life were quieter.

The art world had moved on. New movements were emerging. Her name appeared less frequently in newspapers. But she kept painting altars, landscapes, small domestic scenes—work filled with a kind of distilled serenity.

The theatrics of earlier years gave way to something gentler, more contemplative.

She died in 1955, at fifty-three.

By then, Kahlo had been mythologized, Rivera had been canonized, and the muralist movement had been enshrined as the official visual language of twentieth-century Mexico.

María Izquierdo did not fit neatly into this story, so she was pushed to its margins.

But margins, as scholars now like to say, are where the real history ferments.

And María Izquierdo is, without question, one of the most important Mexican painters of the twentieth century—not because she matched the era, but because she insisted on painting the parts of Mexican life that the era chose to ignore.

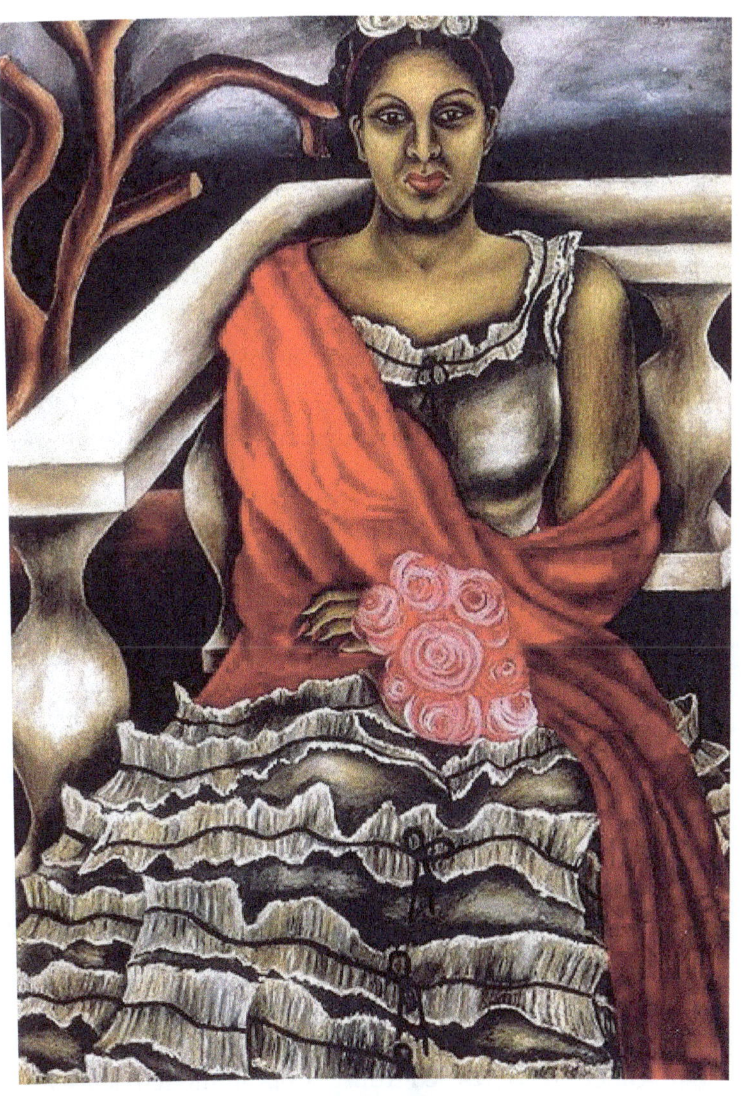

Retrato, 1940

Being Maria

There is a moment in every artist's life when the external narrative—exhibitions, lovers, scandals, movements—falls away, and what remains is simply the work and the person capable of making it.

With María Izquierdo, that moment happens somewhere in the mid-1930s, when she is in her early thirties and standing squarely at the hinge between a Mexico inventing itself for the twentieth century and the private universe that she, almost alone, insisted on painting.

People often say Mexican art of the period was "nationalist," a word that usually suggests flags, heroes, and murals the size of mountainsides. But nationalism can also be a quieter thing: a set of symbols passed through memory, a personal devotion repurposed into a public language.

María understood this instinctively. She did not need a manifesto, or a party affiliation, or a government-commissioned wall to participate in the making of modern Mexican identity.

She only needed her imagination.

And in the 1930s, that imagination was on fire.

It is tempting to see her circus paintings as a genre experiment, something borrowed from European modernism—the Degas dancers, the Picasso harlequins. Critics make this comparison often; some do it lazily, as if any woman painter who paints a performer must be in conversation with Paris.

But the Mexican circus of María's generation was not the Belle Époque spectacle of silk tights and powdered wigs. It was rougher, stranger, itinerant: a collection of bodies, animals, and illusions traveling across landscapes still marked by the Revolution's scars.

Imagine an old tent pitched at the edge of a small town in Coahuila. The air smells like sweat and peanuts and the dry metallic tang of desert dust. Children press against the tent flaps. A clown paints his face in the corner, and the paint melts slightly in the heat. A horse stamps its hoof. A woman in sequins tests the strength of a rope with her palm. Everything is anticipation.

This is the circus María saw.

Her performers are not idealized; they are vulnerable. The balancing acts seem perilous, the fiestas slightly worn. Some of the clowns look like men who have seen too much. Her palette in these paintings—warm ochres, reds, blues—feels like a stage lit by lanterns rather than electric bulbs.

What María found in the circus was not spectacle but metaphor.

A body suspended in midair is a body negotiating the terms of its own survival. This was an image she understood intimately.

It is no accident that many of her circus paintings date from her years with Tamayo, or that they rise in intensity after she leaves the academy. Domestic life had a perimeter; the circus had none. It was transitory, improvised, theatrical, and yet profoundly disciplined. For a woman who had walked out of one life and into another, the circus offered a structure for imagining freedom.

Then there are the women at windows—figures caught between interior and exterior, between the sanctity of home and the world just beyond reach. These images recur throughout her work. Sometimes the woman looks out with longing, other times with resignation. But the window is always a threshold, and María's windows are never simply architectural; they are psychological apertures.

The window is the space where desire meets possibility. It is the place where a woman asks herself whether to stay or to leave.

María left many things in her life—husbands, schools, movements, expectations. The windows in her paintings are reminders of every departure and every return.

One of the most quietly radical aspects of María Izquierdo's work is her treatment of objects. She paints them with the same emotional intensity that other artists reserve for human subjects. A watermelon, a ceramic jar, a paper banner, a rope, a mask—these do not sit inert on a table. They are charged, sometimes ominous, sometimes tender.

She once said, "Objects have a soul," which sounds mystical until you remember she grew up in a world where an altar could bring someone to tears, where a candle's flicker could stand in for a prayer, where the line between the sacred and the ordinary was thin enough to tear with a breath.

In her still lifes, the objects are never fully still. They lean, they listen, they seem to wait for something unnamed. Art historians sometimes call these works "folk modernism," a term that feels both accurate and insufficient. Izquierdo was not painting folklore; she was painting memory. And memory is never literal—it rearranges itself according to emotional necessity.

Consider her 1940s altar paintings. At first glance, they look like straightforward depictions of household shrines—veladoras, papel picado, saints, offerings of fruit. But look again. The space is too perfect, too symmetrical, too quiet. The shadows fall with the deliberateness of theatrical lighting. The fruits feel expectant. There is a tension in these compositions, as if the entire scene has been assembled for an event that refuses to begin.

Altars are, in Mexican culture, sites of communication with the dead. María's altars feel like conversations with the parts of her life she could no longer reach—the girlhood interrupted, the marriage left behind, the mural she was denied, the future that always shimmered slightly out of view.

Every artist has an interior landscape. For María, that landscape was furnished with objects carrying emotional weight.

A jar is never just a jar.

A ribbon is never just a ribbon.

A rope is never just a rope.

In one late painting, the rope hangs visibly cut—an unmistakable evocation of her mural commission stolen from her by Rivera and Siqueiros. The tragedy of that moment reappears symbolically again and again, the rope always severed, the act always unfinished.

Perhaps the most overtly psychological work in her career is *Sueño y premonición*, painted in 1947. This is the one with the woman standing beside her own severed head—a composition so startling that even now it shakes viewers out of complacency.

Scholars often interpret the painting as autobiographical, but it is important to remember: María rarely painted literal autobiography. What she painted were psychological states, the internal weather systems of a woman absorbing loss, ambition, criticism, desire, and betrayal all at once.

The woman in the painting stands calm, composed, almost resigned—her severed head resting at her feet like something shed, not violently torn. Behind her, a tower burns. The sky is darkening. The composition has the logical illogic of dreams, where symbolism arrives heavy and uninvited.

What is the dream, and what is the premonition?

Which is past, and which is future?

What part of yourself must you lose to enter the next version of your life?

These are the questions the painting asks.

This was painted two years after her mural commission was revoked. It was also painted at a moment when she sensed her body beginning to change in ways she couldn't fully name. The stroke that would compromise her right side was not far off.

If Part I of María's life is about breaking free, then Part II is about living inside that freedom—its rewards, its dangers, its solitude.

Freedom is not always gentle.

Often it is a landscape full of sharp edges.

Though she is less known for her portraiture than Kahlo, María did paint people—friends, fellow artists, anonymous women, children. But her portraits do something unusual: they flatten affect in a way that paradoxically exposes the sitter's emotional life more fully.

Her subjects look directly out of the canvas, neither smiling nor performing. There is an almost ethnographic stillness to them—not in the sense of classification, but in the sense of attention. María wasn't interested in capturing likeness alone; she was painting states of being.

In *Retrato de Belem*, the young woman sits before us with an expression that hovers between solemnity and defiance. She is centered, dignified, and entirely present. María does not embellish her. She does not dramatize her. She lets her be.

This is, in its way, the most radical feminist gesture of all.

To paint a woman as a person rather than a symbol.

To paint her as self-possessed rather than decorative.

To refuse the ornamental.

Where Rivera monumentalized women as allegories of the nation, and Kahlo dramatized the body as a theater of pain, María painted women with a directness that feels startlingly contemporary. Her feminism was not theoretical; it was in her brush.

By the late 1930s and early 1940s, María was successful—exhibiting in the United States, Europe, and South America. She had patrons, supporters, and a reputation for fierce independence. Yet she also lived with fragility—emotional, financial, relational.

The break with Tamayo, though not catastrophic, left her navigating the art world alone.

She entered another relationship, with the painter Raúl Uribe, who would remain with her for the rest of her life. But companionship does not erase loneliness, and María's diaries from the period (the few that survive) suggest a woman wrestling with doubt.

Artists are often imagined as creatures of certainty, but María was full of questions about her work and how it would fit into the world:

Was her work understood?
Would it last?
Would she be remembered?
Was she painting the right things?

These are the questions you can feel hovering behind her canvases, especially the ones that carry tension rather than clarity.

The Mexican art world of the time was notoriously hierarchical. The muralists occupied the top rung; women were expected to remain on the bottom. María refused this structure, but refusing a hierarchy does not exempt you from its effects. She faced condescension, dismissal, outright hostility.

Critics wrote about her in tones that suggested her success was accidental. A few praised her vision but always with the faint stench of paternalism.

And yet she kept painting with a stubbornness that feels admirable, even heroic.

She painted when she was poor.

She painted when she was tired.
She painted when she was sick.
She painted when she was ignored.
She painted when she was betrayed.
She painted when the art world tried to shut her out.

Art was not her profession; it was her identity.

By the mid-1940s, a shift is visible in her work. The colors darken slightly. The compositions grow more introspective. The symbolic objects remain, but they seem to cluster more tightly, as if the world were closing in.

Then came the stroke.

It is impossible to overstate the cruelty of this moment for an artist whose life had been carved from refusal.

The body that had carried her away from marriage, through motherhood, into the capital, into the academy, out of the academy, through years of painting, through betrayal, into exhibitions—this body suddenly refused to cooperate.

Her right side weakened. Her speech was affected. And yet she continued to work, teaching herself to paint with her left hand, adjusting her technique, simplifying forms, slowing her pace.

It was not a defeat.

It was an adaptation.

In the last decade of her life, her paintings become quieter, filled with empty rooms, still altars, landscapes with long horizons. The theatricality of her earlier work remains, but it softens around the edges.

She is no longer painting the struggle to claim space; she is painting the space she has claimed.

There is a kind of peace in these works—though not a passive peace. It is the peace of a woman who has lived entirely on her own terms, even when those terms came with cost.

Her final paintings feel like the closing of a long, complicated prayer.

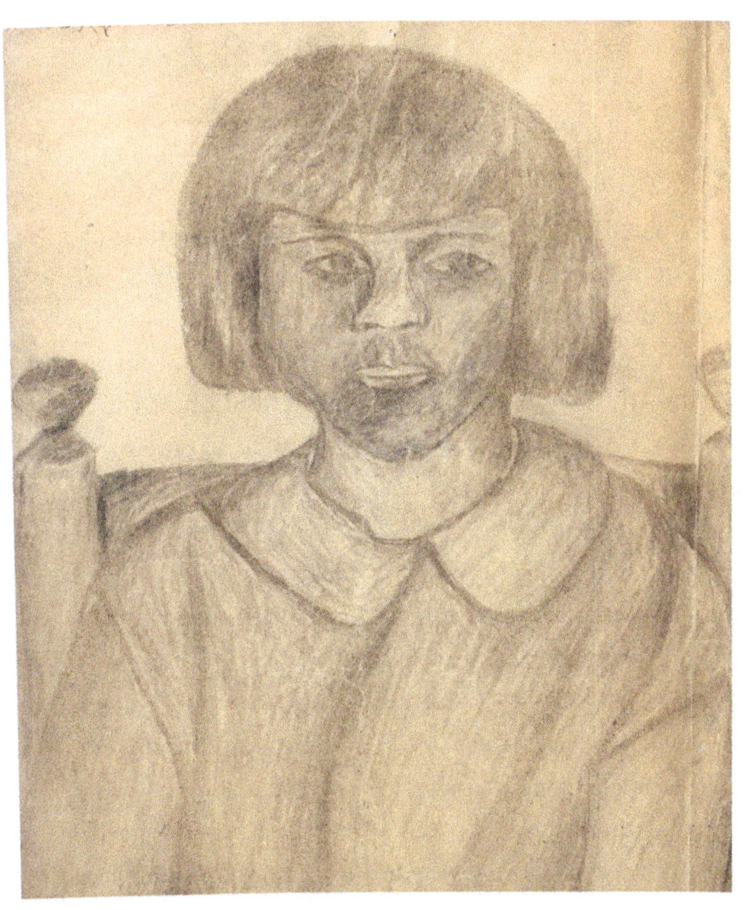

Retrato de niña, 1931

The Reckoning

For a long time after her death in 1955, María Izquierdo's name lived in the shadows of the murals and the male-dominated canon of Mexican modernism. But like many exiled voices, her work waited, silent but durable, until the world tired of its old stories.

The first major breath of rediscovery came in the late 1980s. In 1988–1989, a significant exhibition at the Centro Cultural Arte Contemporáneo in Mexico City reintroduced her to a new generation of Mexican viewers. Paintings such as *"Retrato de Amparo, la hija de la artista"* (1951) re-emerged from private collections; works once relegated to dusty corners of memory again hung under museum lights.

Not long before, in 1983, one of her paintings — *"Los peregrinos"* (1945) — had been shown at the Instituto Nacional de Bellas Artes. Through these exhibitions, curators and scholars began to ask: why had she been sidelined for so long? And what did it mean — in the history of Mexican art — to neglect the only woman of her generation who had really insisted on creating from her own vision?

Once the conversation reopened, it didn't stop. Her paintings, long scattered in private holdings or tucked away in lesser-known collections, began circulating. Museums re-acquired altars, circus-themed canvases, still lifes, portraits. The aesthetic tenderness and symbolic weight of scenes like *"Viernes de Dolores"* (1944–45), which depicts a traditional altar with candles, fruit, papel picado and devotional offering, gained renewed appreciation.

The effect was cumulative. By the 1990s and early 2000s, galleries in the United States began to show her work. A landmark moment was the exhibition The True Poetry: The Art of María Izquierdo (September 27–December 28, 1990) at the Americas Society in New York. That show brought together more than fifty of her paintings and works on paper, drawn from both Mexican and U.S. public and private collections. It traveled to other venues, including a West Coast stop, giving new visibility to an artist once confined to footnotes.

Within Mexico, the recognition reached a symbolic peak on 25 October 2002 — the centenary of her birth — when she was declared a "Monumento Artístico de la Nación." That legal and cultural designation guaranteed that her work would be catalogued, preserved, and protected.

By the early 21st century, Izquierdo's name no longer belonged to obscure scholarship alone. Her paintings began entering public museum collections; altars, still lifes, and portraits once considered "folk," peripheral or domestic, came to be understood as central to modernism's full scope.

What stands out now — nearly a century since her first solo exhibition — is how varied and resilient María's work remains.

Take *"Retrato de Belem"* (1928), the portrait of her half-sister, which featured in her first solo show in November 1929 at the Galería de Arte Moderno inside the then-Teatro Nacional (today the Palacio de Bellas Artes). The portrait — the sitter in burgundy dress beside a wooden dresser — already shows the sculptural solidity and calm dignity that would become a signature of her portraiture.

At the other end of her life sits *"Sueño y presentimiento"* (1947), one of her most haunting works. In it a female figure — often read as a stand-in for the artist — appears in a spectral landscape, clutching a severed head that resembles her own. It is a painting that refuses the melodramatic flash of a self-portrait and instead offers a nightmare turned sacred. Art historians today see this not simply as a personal catharsis but as a symbolic, almost ritualistic reckoning with loss, betrayal, and existential disquiet — a stark, uncompromising vision of a life that refused easy closure.

In between these, there are the circus paintings, which are no longer curiosities or niche interests but considered some of the most original articulations of female agency in Mexican modernism. *"Los caballitos pony en su camerino"* (1945) — a view behind the performance tent, showing a costumed woman and ornately decorated ponies — has been auctioned at major houses and is now widely studied.

And then there are the altars. In *"Viernes de Dolores"* (c. 1944–45), the religious devotion of the piece is suffused with earthly brightness: oranges speared with papel picado flags, candles, bowls of sprouting wheat, floral arrangements — all rendered in Izquierdo's characteristic vibrant palette rather than the somber purples often associated with Christian mourning.

Today many of these works are held in major museums and private collections. Institutions like the Museo Blaisten and other public holdings in Mexico preserve her legacy.

Because of this renewed institutional interest, her artwork is no longer an afterthought — curators place Izquierdo alongside, rather than beneath, canonical male painters, arguing that mid-twentieth-century modernism in Mexico loses its fullness if we omit the domestic, devotional, intimate, and feminine registers she documented.

What does it mean to be "influenced" by María Izquierdo in 2025? It doesn't necessarily mean painting like her.

It means — like her — treating everyday objects, home altars, domestic interiors, orphaned memories, and the feminine psyche as legitimate material for art; it means refusing grand narratives and instead privileging intimacy, ambiguity, and emotional truth.

Scholarship has shifted accordingly. Recent studies, such as the 2025 essay Gender, Race and Esotericism in Mexican Visual Art: The Case of María Izquierdo (1902–1955), trace how Izquierdo blended mystical, folkloric, and ancestral imagery in a way that neither romanticized nor exoticized her roots — but insisted they be part of modernism's core.

More artists and curators — especially women, especially Latinx — now see in her a precursor: a model for creative autonomy rooted not in spectacle or propaganda but in the symbolic rhythm of daily life. Her altars anticipate the ritual-inflected installations of artists who work with memory and identity; her portraits, stripped of ornament, speak to a generation tired of performance and eager for presence.

Though direct citations are rare — few younger artists point to her consciously — the aesthetic sensibility is unmistakable. The renewed esteem for domestic scenes, handcrafted objects, vernacular spirituality, and intimate storytelling echoes María's own priorities. The tone may be different; the media may have expanded — photography, installation, mixed media — but the DNA is remarkably similar: art that begins at home, in memory, with the objects we touch every day.

María Izquierdo's journey — from small-town childhood to art student, from scandal and marginalization to rediscovery and reverence — matters because it shows how art history is made and unmade. It shows how power, prejudice, and institutional bias can bury a voice, and how time, technique, and fidelity can resurrect it.

When we look at her paintings now, we don't just see altars or circus scenes or dream landscapes. We see a woman who refused to be defined by someone else's idea of "important art." We see an artist who made the domestic sacred, the humble symbolic, the personal political, without fanfare or mythmaking.

In 2025, as global art looks harder at questions of identity, memory, gender, and marginalization, María Izquierdo stands as a reminder: that the edges often hold the richest detail. That being outside the dominant narrative isn't always a loss — sometimes it's a vantage.

And that a brush, in the right hands, can map an entire unseen world.

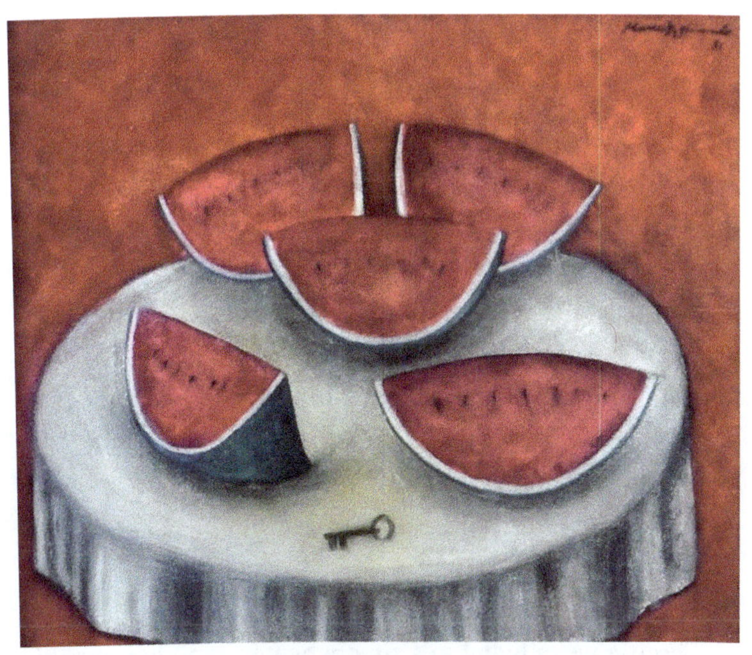

Still Life with Watermelon, 1931

Art Matters

There's a moment — and it always catches you off guard — when you're standing in front of a María Izquierdo painting and the whole atmosphere tilts. The room goes quiet in that way certain truths do.

You realize she's not selling you a nation, or a myth, or a heroic story carved in stone.

She's offering something smaller and heavier: memory arranged on a table.

A color holding a feeling it couldn't say out loud.

A life built out of contradictions she never apologized for.

And that hits different now.

Because we're living in a time when everybody wants big statements, big narratives, big claims. But María was never in that business.

She wasn't trying to shout over the muralists towering above her. She wasn't trying to win the anthem wars. She was building her own world — piece by piece, object by object, vision by vision — and letting that world stand on its own terms.

If you're from Miami, you recognize that move instantly.

It's the same refusal you see in Wynwood before sunrise, when Ahol Sniffs Glue is out there painting those half-lidded eyes, not for the tourists but for the people who actually know what it means to keep watch.

It's in the way Ruben Ubiera paints a kid at a bus stop like he's painting a saint.

It's VantaBlack (Chire Regans) pulling memory out of grief and pinning it to the walls of community centers so nobody gets erased.

It's the dancers in Opa-locka who rehearse behind warehouse windows like they're keeping a quiet promise to themselves.

Maria would've understood that: the idea that the edges are where the real work happens.

And she knew the cost of it too. This was a woman denied a mural because the men in power got nervous when she raised her hand. A woman who painted circus workers not as sideshow "types" but as people with real spines, real sweat, real stories. A woman who painted herself holding her own severed head — not as some surreal stunt, but because she'd lived through enough pressure to know what it feels like to lose pieces of yourself just trying to be heard.

Her art wasn't a thesis. It was survival with style.

And if you look around today — at the scene, the music, the under-the-radar brilliance happening in backyards and block parties and makeshift studios — you see how much of her spirit is still moving.

Think about Denzel Curry, pouring psychic weight and Florida heat into tracks that feel like dream-reports. Or the way Ivy Queen can light up a tiny room and make everyone in it feel like they're inside a ritual, not a performance. Or those nights with DJ Spam Allstars, where the beat pulls ancestors into the present without making a speech about it.

These artists aren't "outsiders."
They're just not waiting on permission.

Which is exactly what María practiced long before the word "decolonial" showed up on museum banners. She took the so-called minor things — a table set for a feast day, an altar built with everyday objects, a woman staring back at you like she already understands every box you're about to put her in — and she made them major. She didn't need the cathedral scale. She made the domestic into a revolution.

If her legacy feels clearer now, it's not because she changed.

It's because we finally learned how to look.

Her paintings don't rise like a shout; they settle like sediment. Slow. Patient. A kind of truth that builds in layers until suddenly you realize: oh — there it is. The real story. Not the official one. The lived one.

A fruit on a table becomes a whole cosmology.

A portrait becomes a negotiation.

A quiet object becomes proof that the rituals of ordinary people outlast the systems that try to flatten them.

I don't want to wrap her up with some tidy line about justice or recognition. That's not how art history works. And anyway, she was never asking for closure.

What she leaves us is a stance.

A way of seeing.

A refusal to shrink the self.

A belief that what's close to the body — what's carried, held, repeated — matters more than whatever story the official voices are selling.

That's the inheritance.

It's not loud, but it lasts.
And honestly?
For someone like me — someone who's spent years painting walls, restoring frescoes, spinning beats all night, and, most importantly, learning from the artists the canon tries to forget — that kind of legacy is the one that hits home the hardest.

PLATES

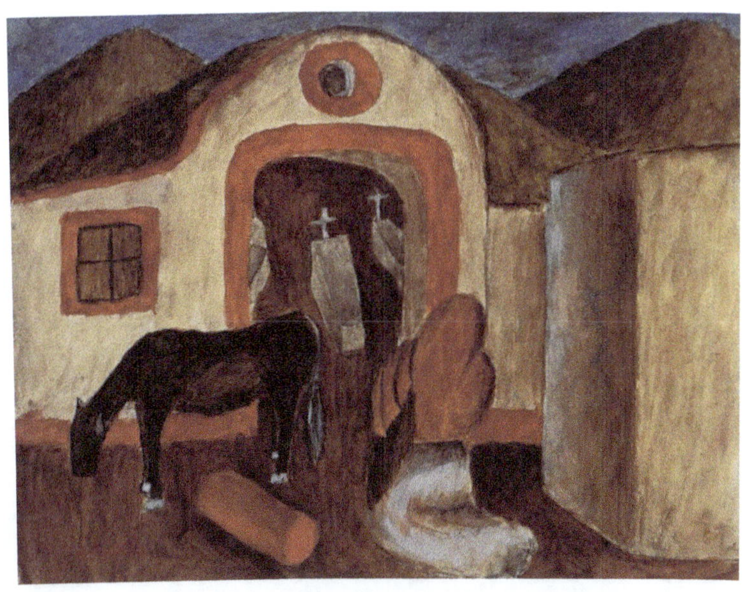

Calvario (Calvary), 1933

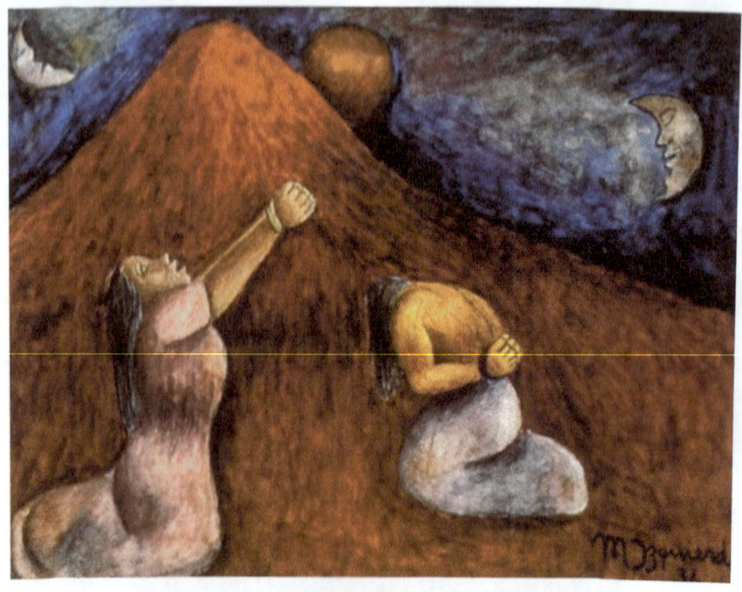

Slaves in a Mythical Landscape, 1936

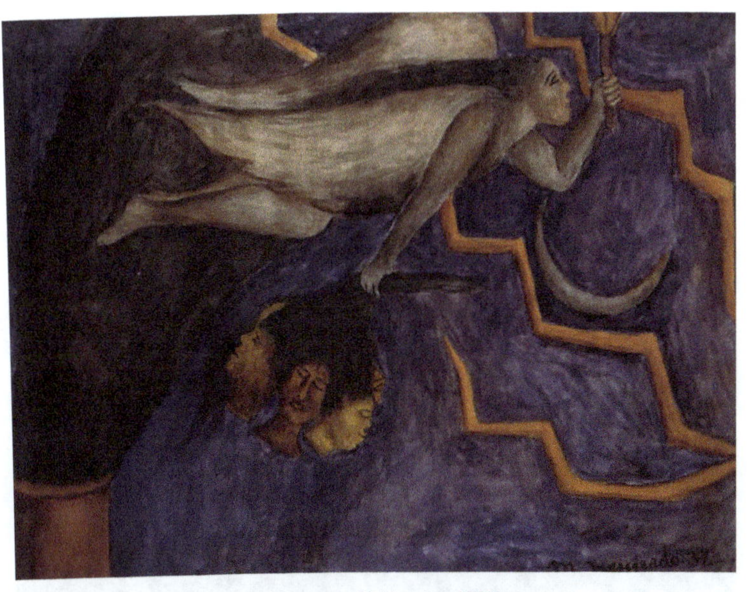

Allegory of Liberty, 1937

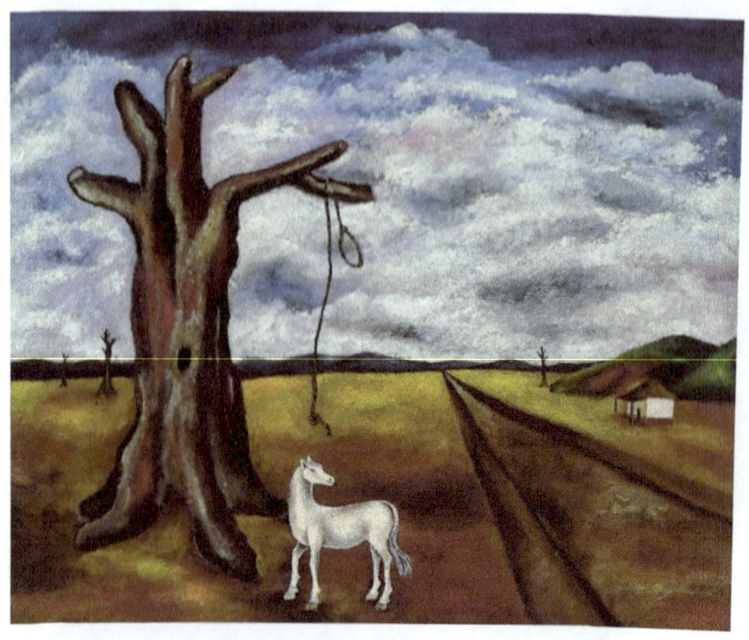

La Soga (The Rope), 1937

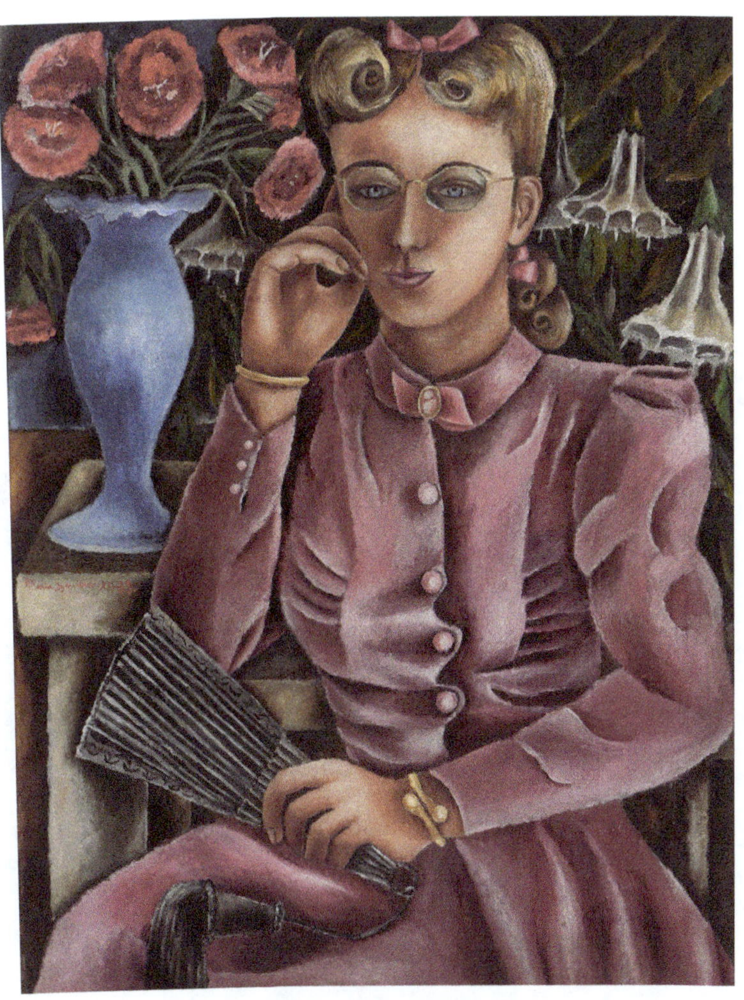

Portrait of Cathie, 1939

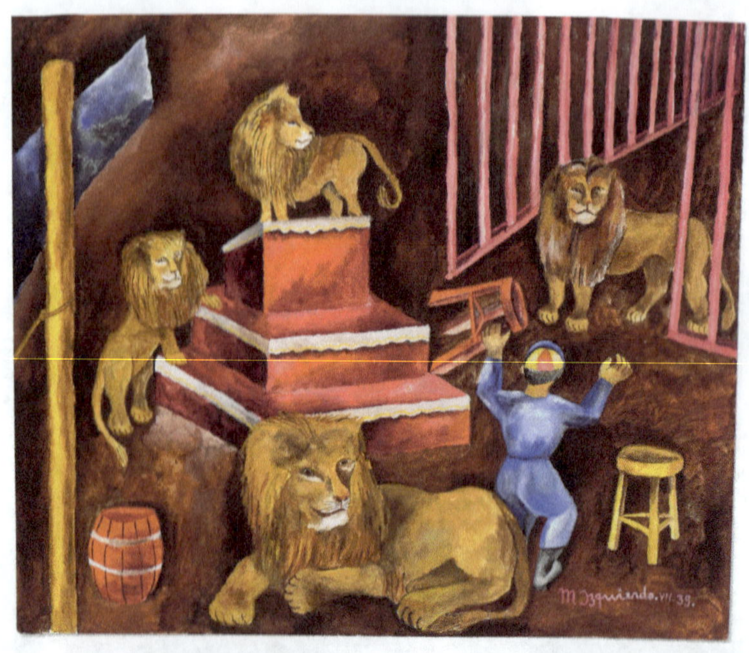

El domador (also known as Leones), 1939

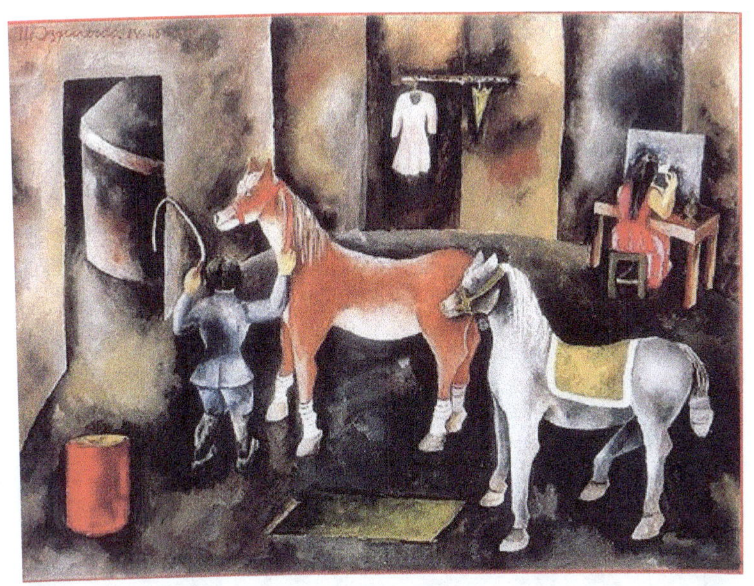

Circus, 1940

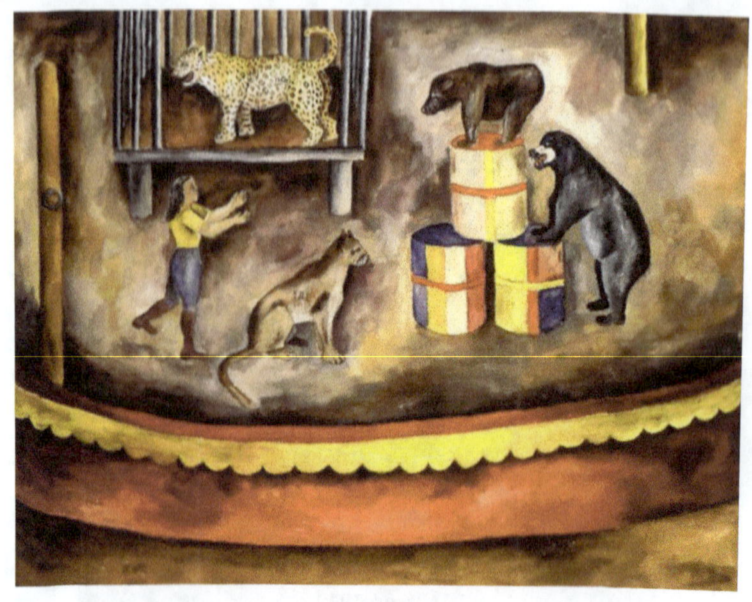

Circus, 1940

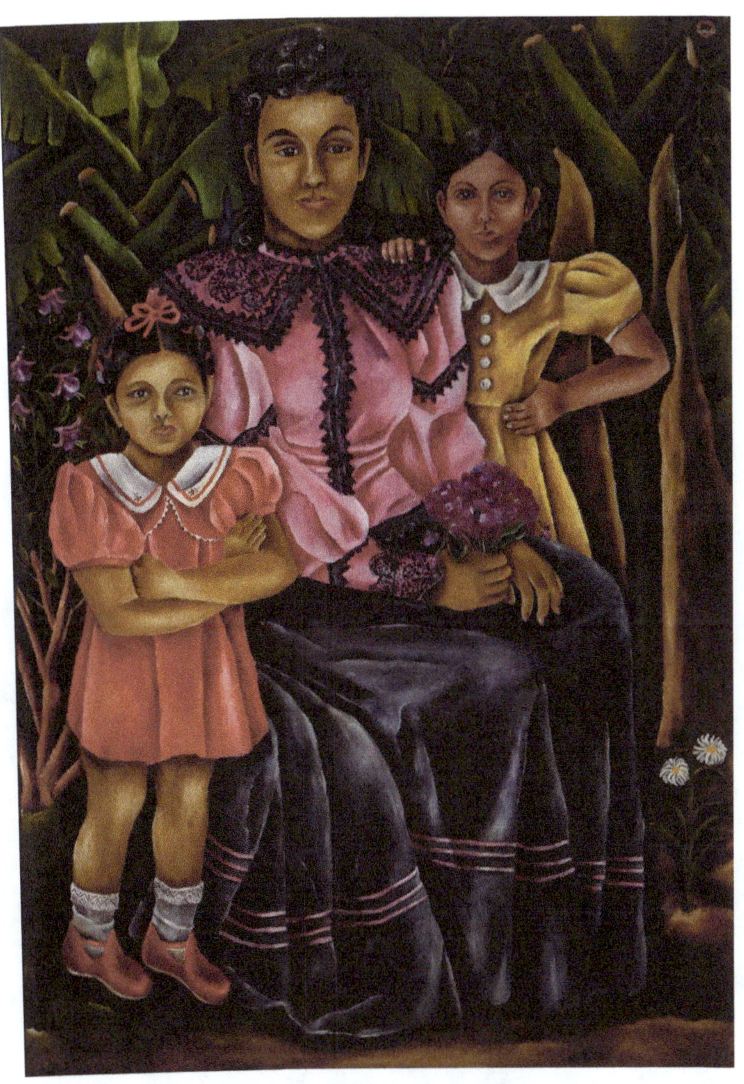

Mis sobrinas (My nieces), 1940

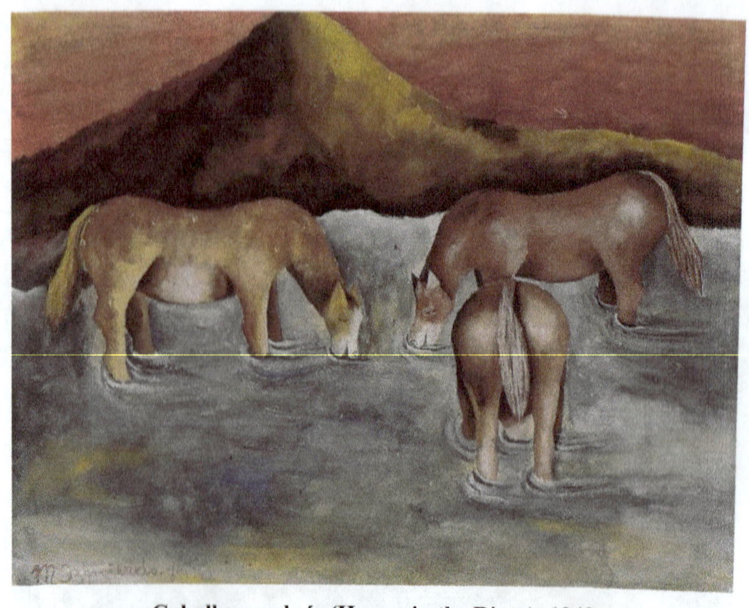

Caballos en el río (Horses in the River), 1940

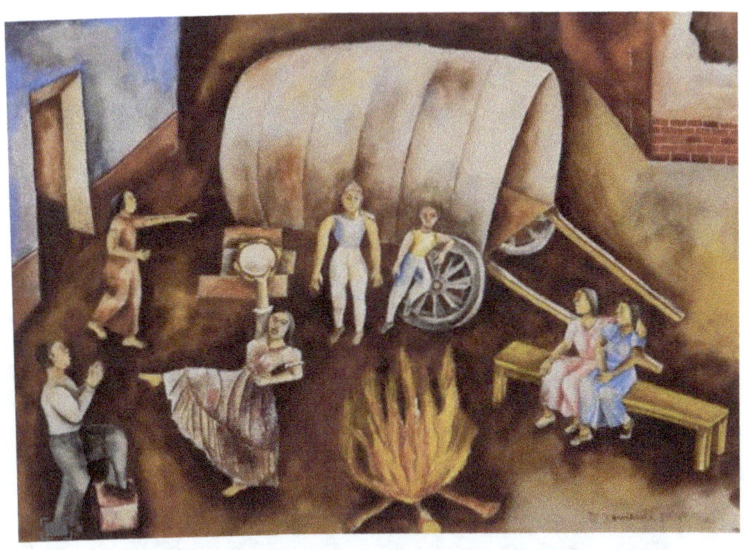

Escena de circo con gitana (Circus with Gypsies), 1940

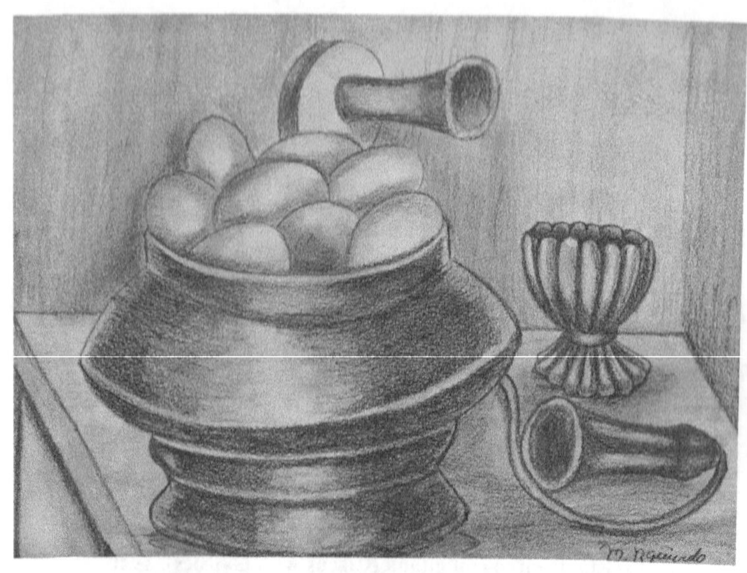

untitled drawing, 1942

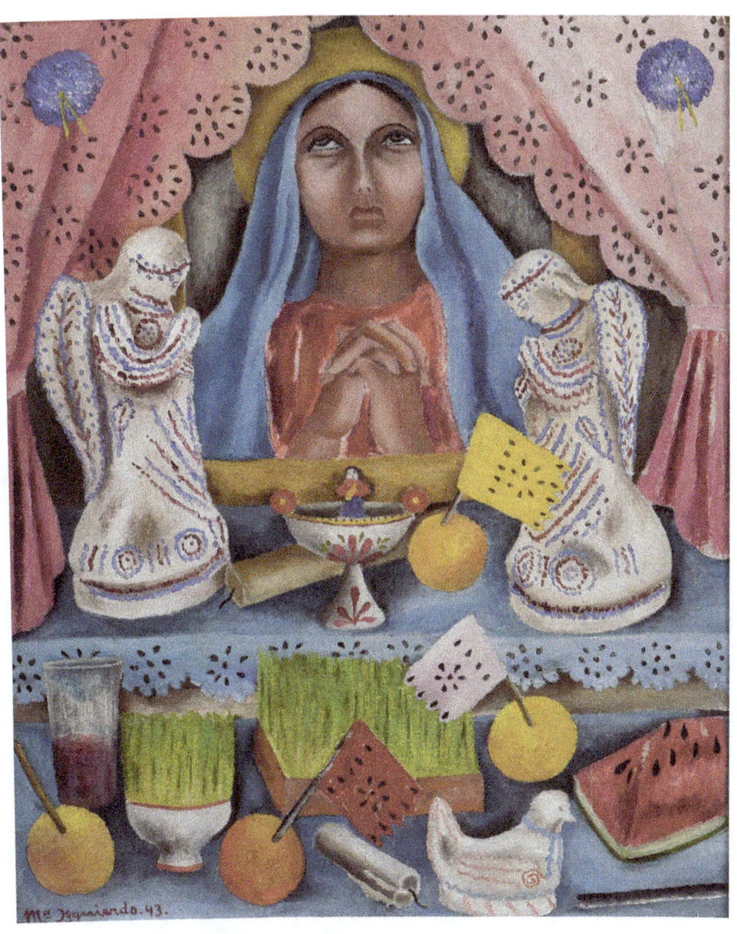

Our Lady of Sorrows, 1943

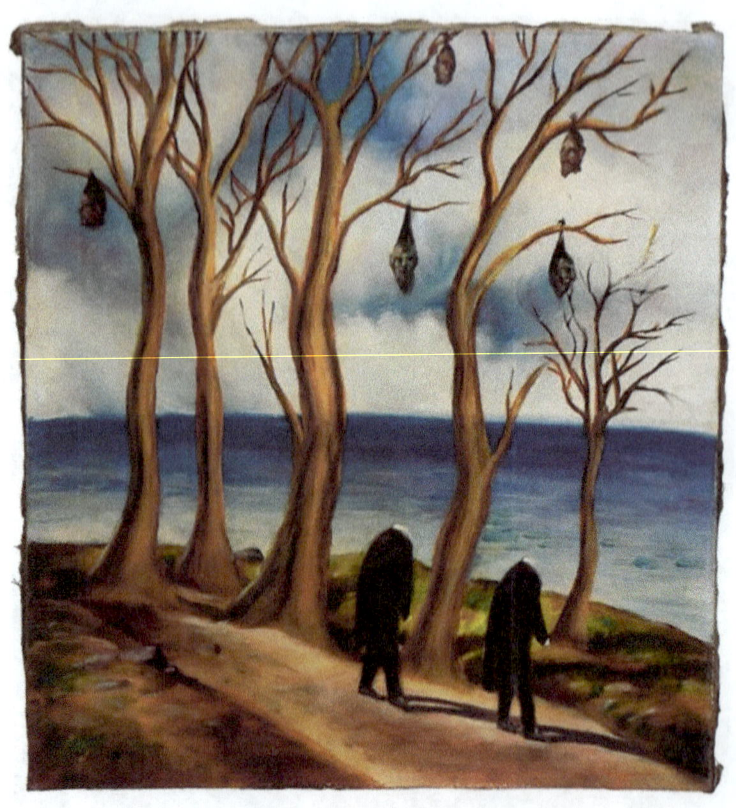

Frutas extrañas, 1943

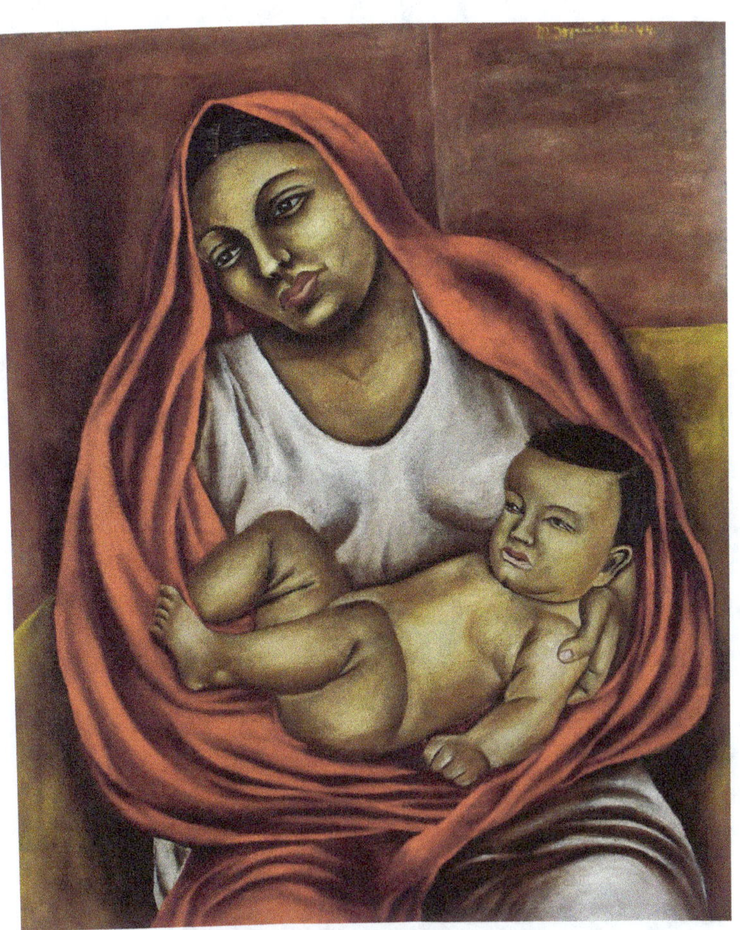

Oil on composition board 55 1/10" × 39 2/5"

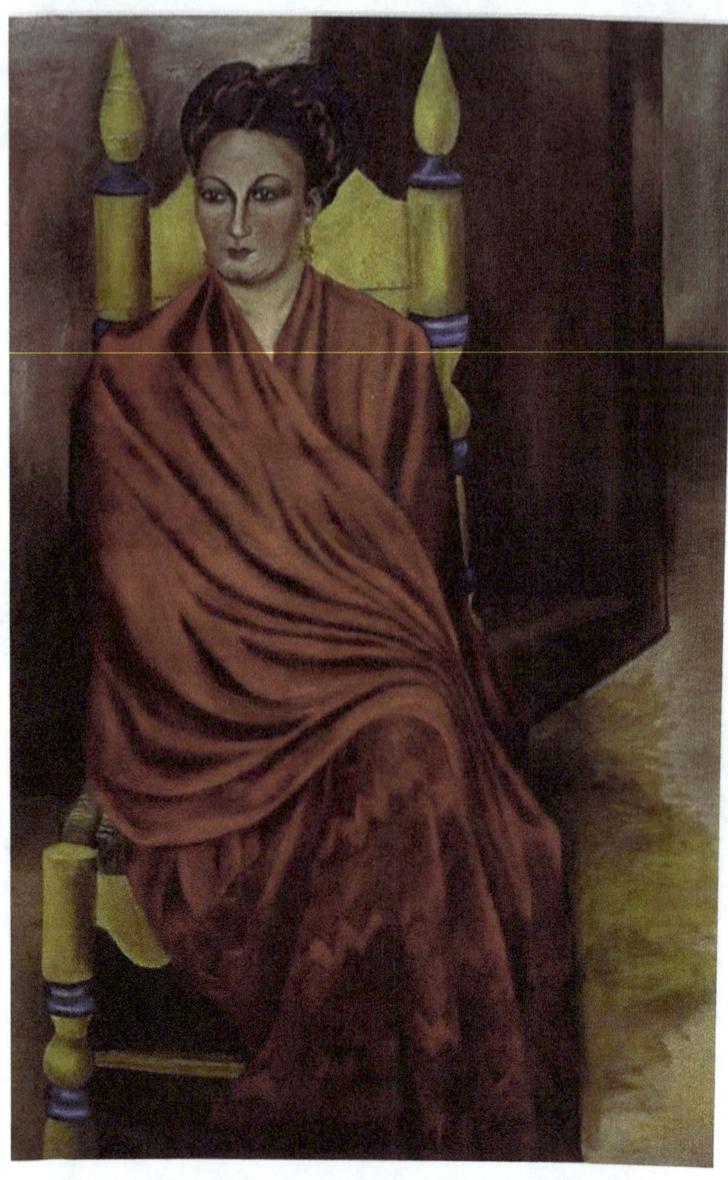

Rebozo rojo (possible portrait of Sra. María Luisa Vargas de Domínguez), 1944

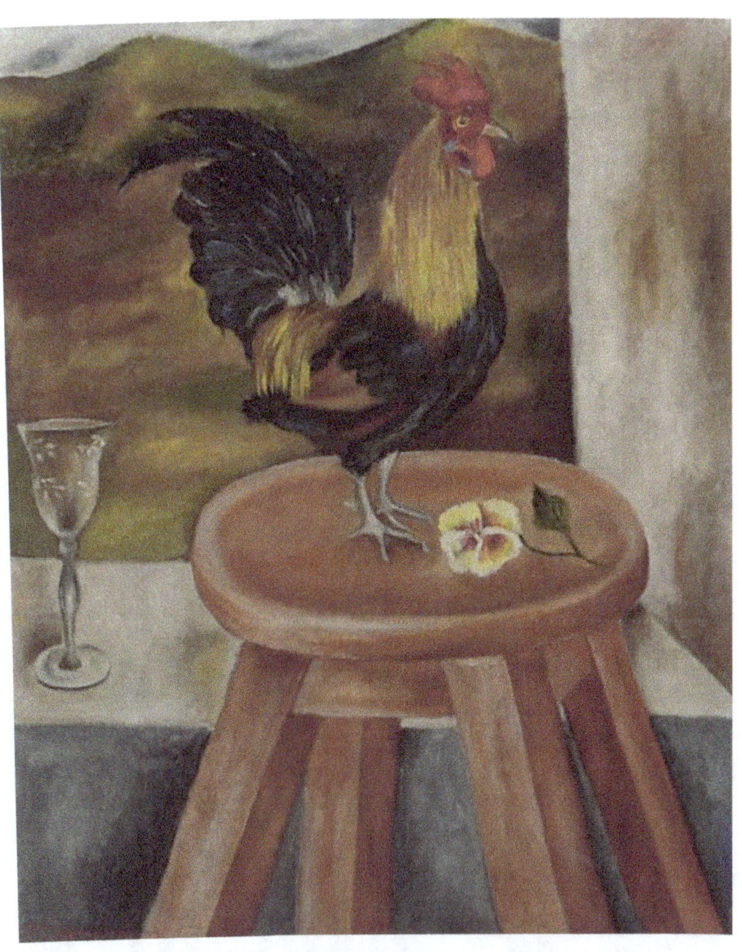

El Gallo, 1945

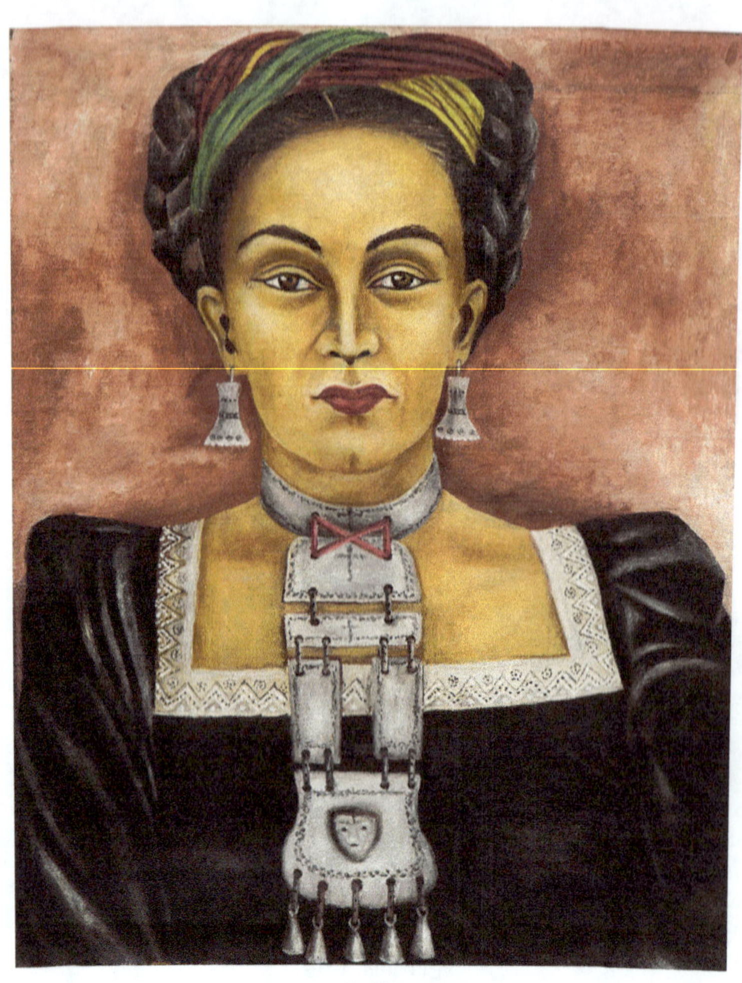

Autorretrato (Self Portrait), 1946

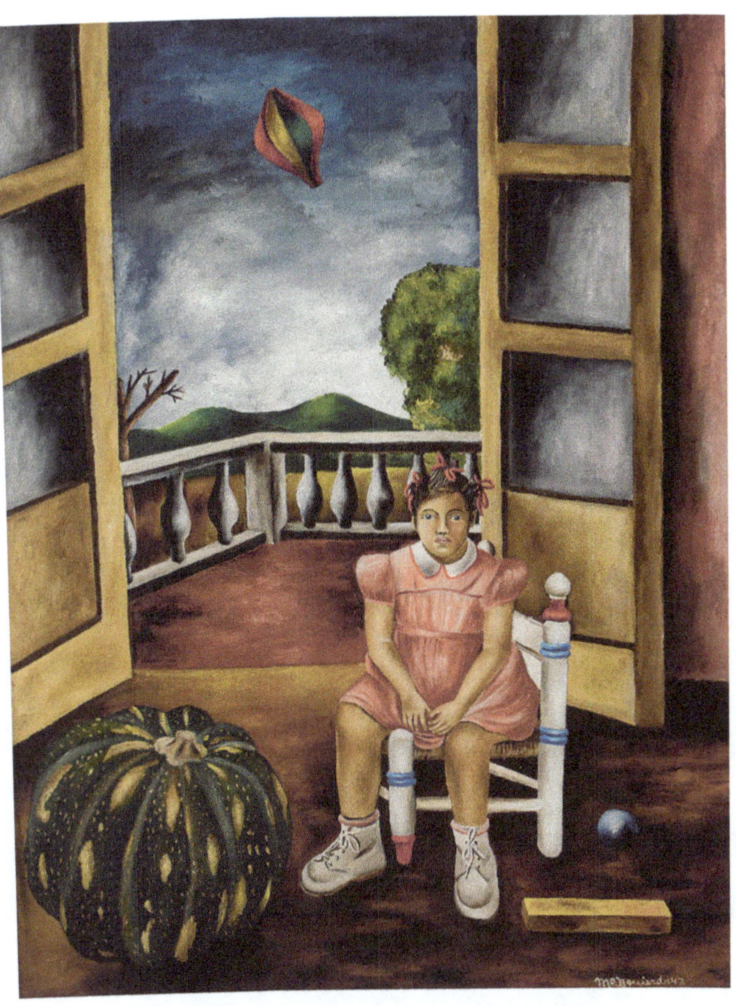

La nina indifférente (The indifferent girl), 1946

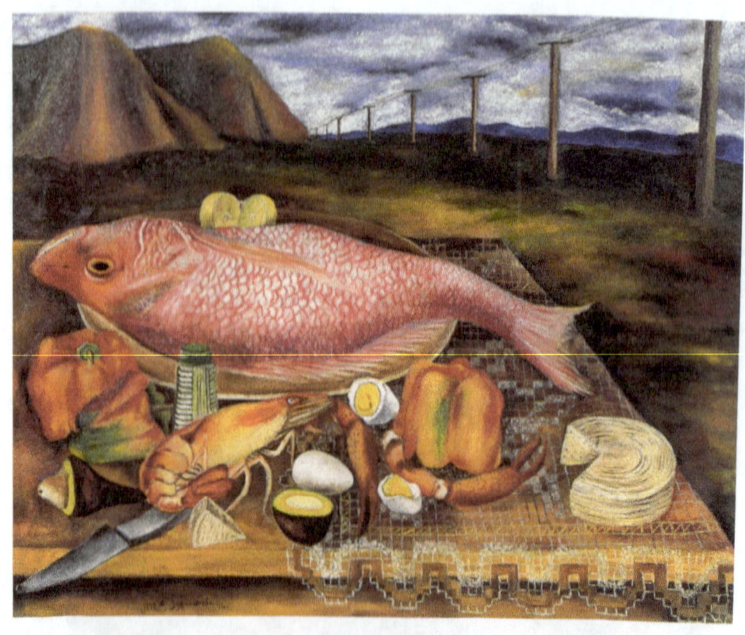

Naturaleza viva con huachinango (Still life with Red Snapper), 1946

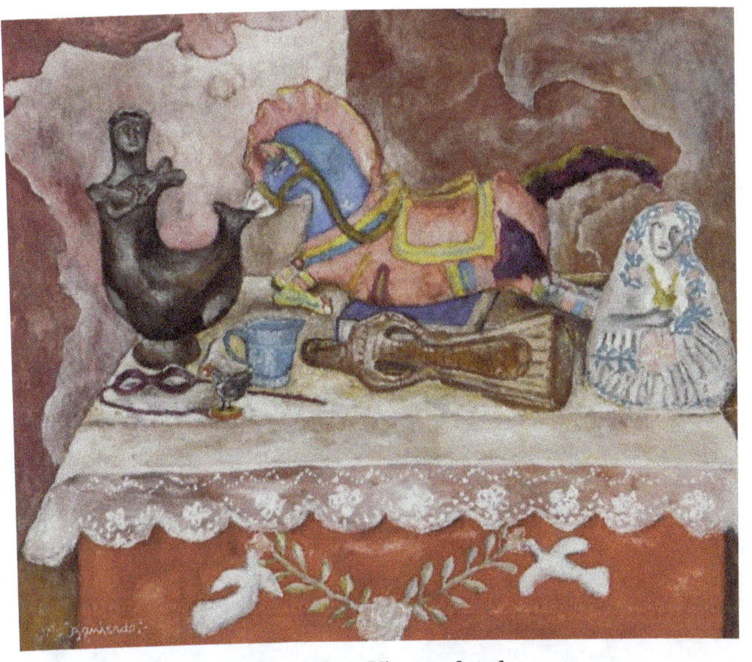

Naturaleza Viva, undated

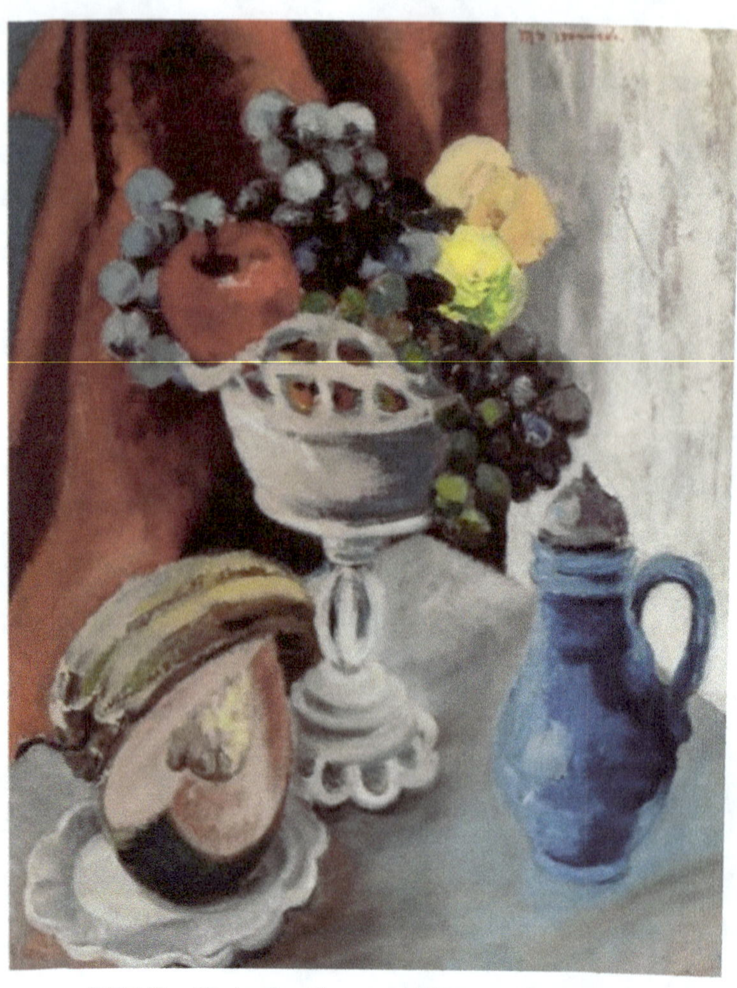

Still Life with Apples, Grapes and Melon, unknown year

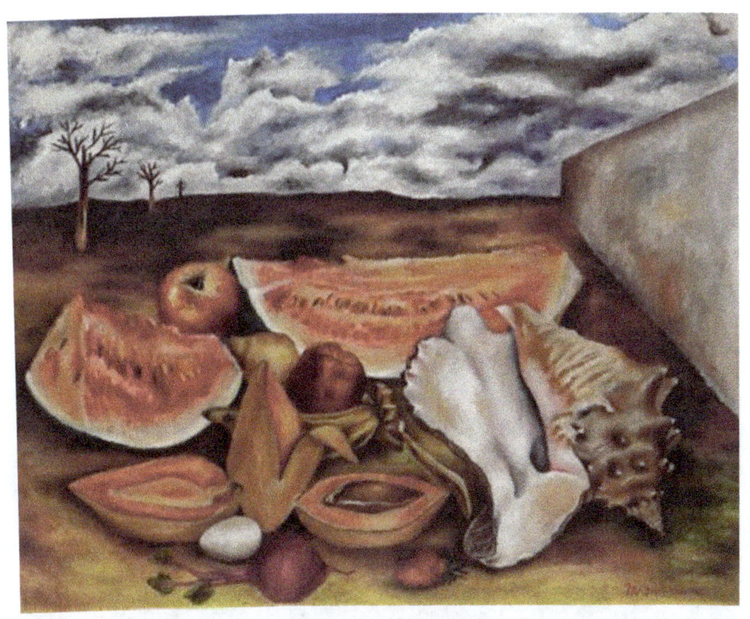

Still Life, 1946

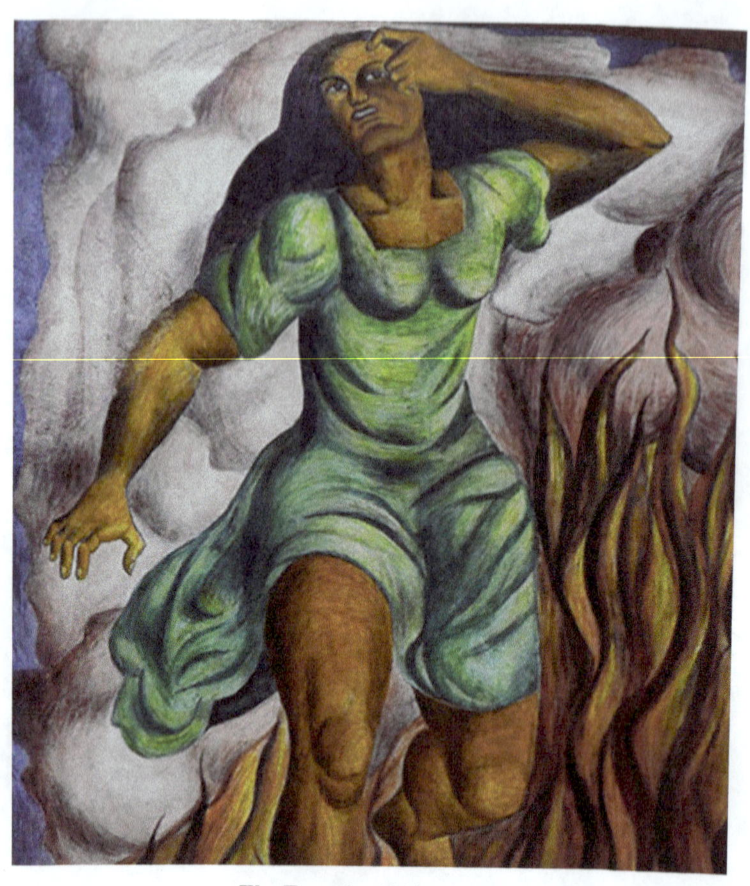

The Tragedy, 1946 (mural)

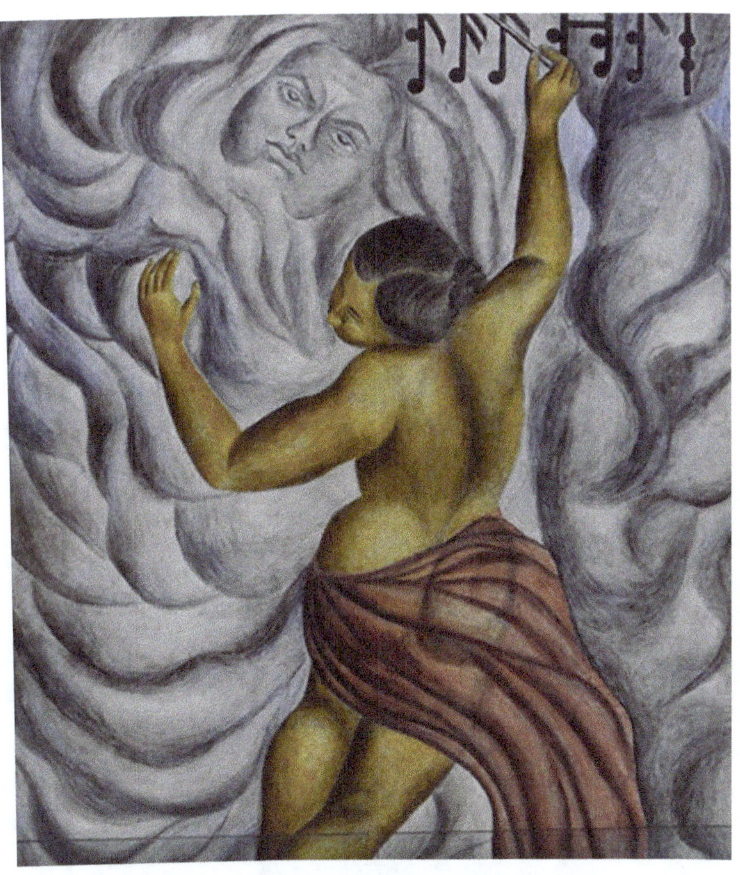

The Music, 1946 (mural)

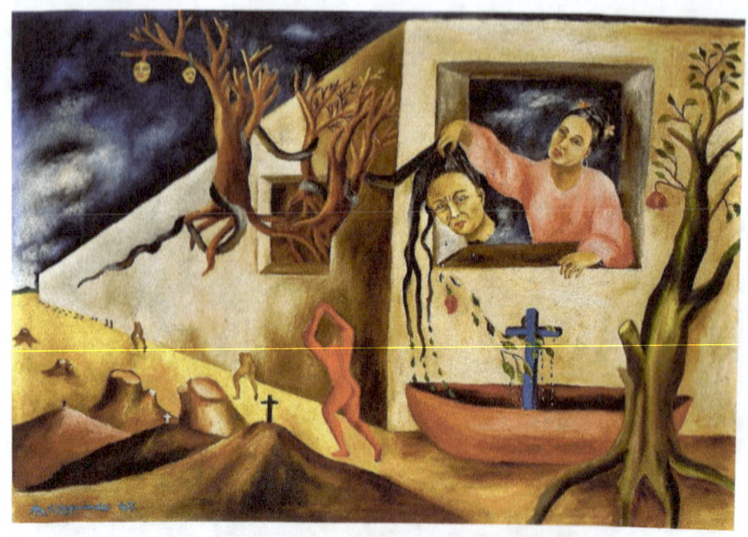

Dream and Premonition, 1947

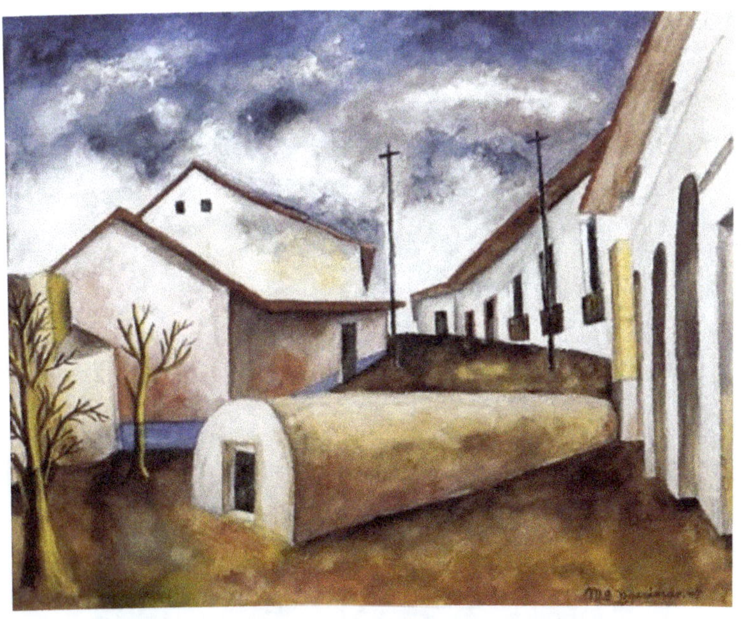

Paisaje de Patzcuaro (Landscape of Patzcuaro), 1947

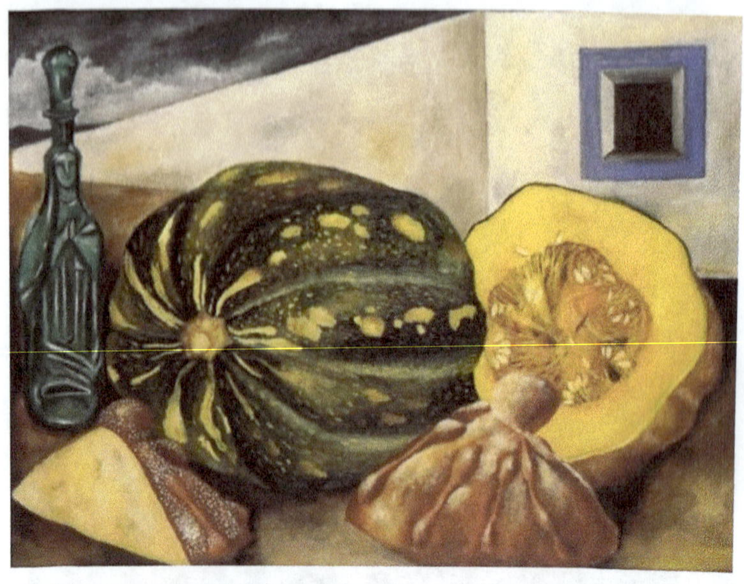

Calabazas con Pan de Muerto (Pumpkin with Day of the Dead Bread), 1947

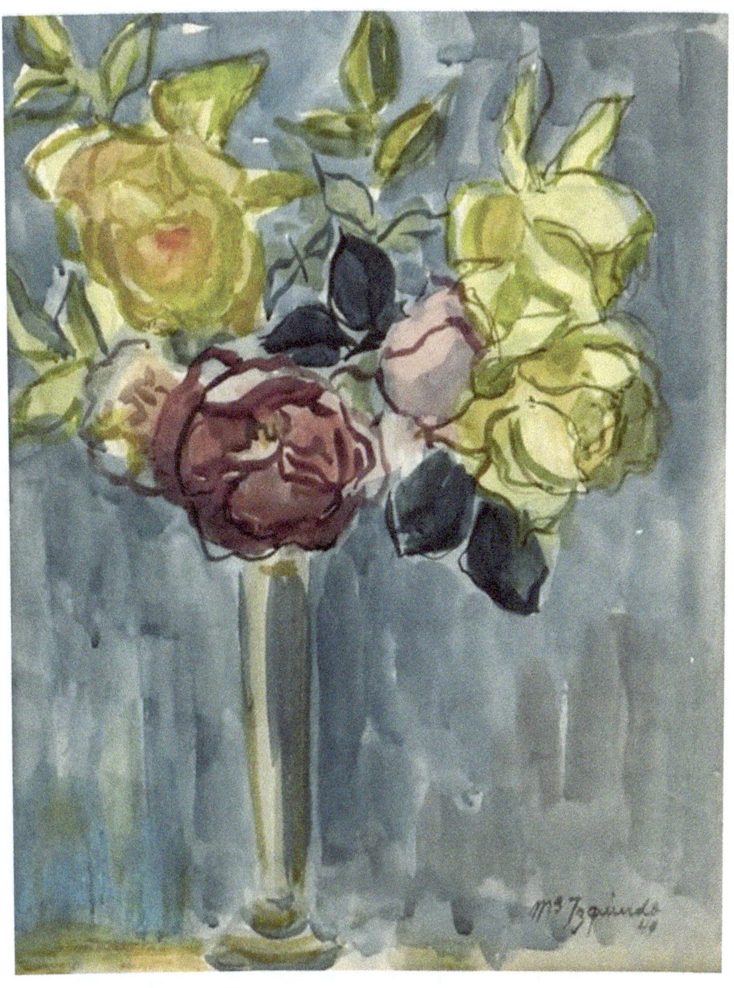

Still Life, 1949

Blaze Carter is a Miami-based visual artist, writer, and musician whose work blends classical training and contemporary street art.

Trained in art restoration with a foundation in the European classics, he has built a career exploring overlooked artists across all genres, bringing his own interests in graffiti and the rhythms of hip-hop into dialogue with historical art.

Carter's interests lie in recasting the canon for today, tracing connections between street art, ritual, memory, nationalism, and the work of artists who have been marginalized or forgotten. As a musician, he brings the improvisational energy of hip-hop to both his writing and his painting, examining how culture, performance, and everyday experience shape the stories we tell about art.

He lives and works in Miami, continuing to create, restore, decolonize, perform, and write, always attentive to the overlooked, the intimate, and the quietly transformative.

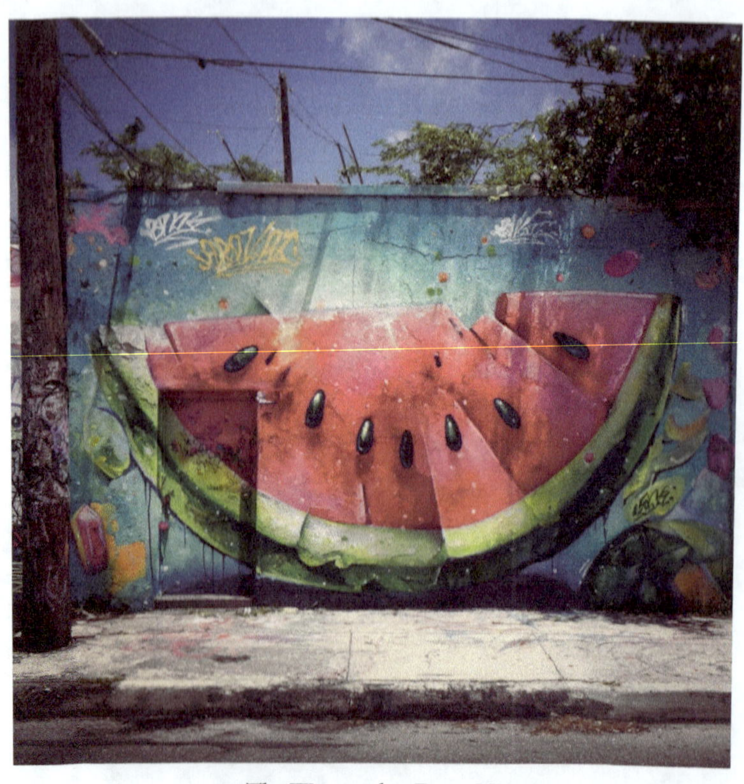

The Watermelon Door, Miami

Blaze Carter

www.ingramcontent.com/pod-product-compliance
Lightning Source LLC
Chambersburg PA
CBHW051511050726
47594CB00010B/4051